The Alphabutt Book

An ABCs of Baby Butts & Bodies

A
is for

Avocado Butt

And all the awesome acrobatic-y things it can achieve

Teresa Bellón • @teresa_bellon

B is for Button Butt

Bouncing blissfully before a big ol' bubble bath

Gemma Correll • @gemmacorrell

is for

Chasing chatty chihuahuas in Chattanooga

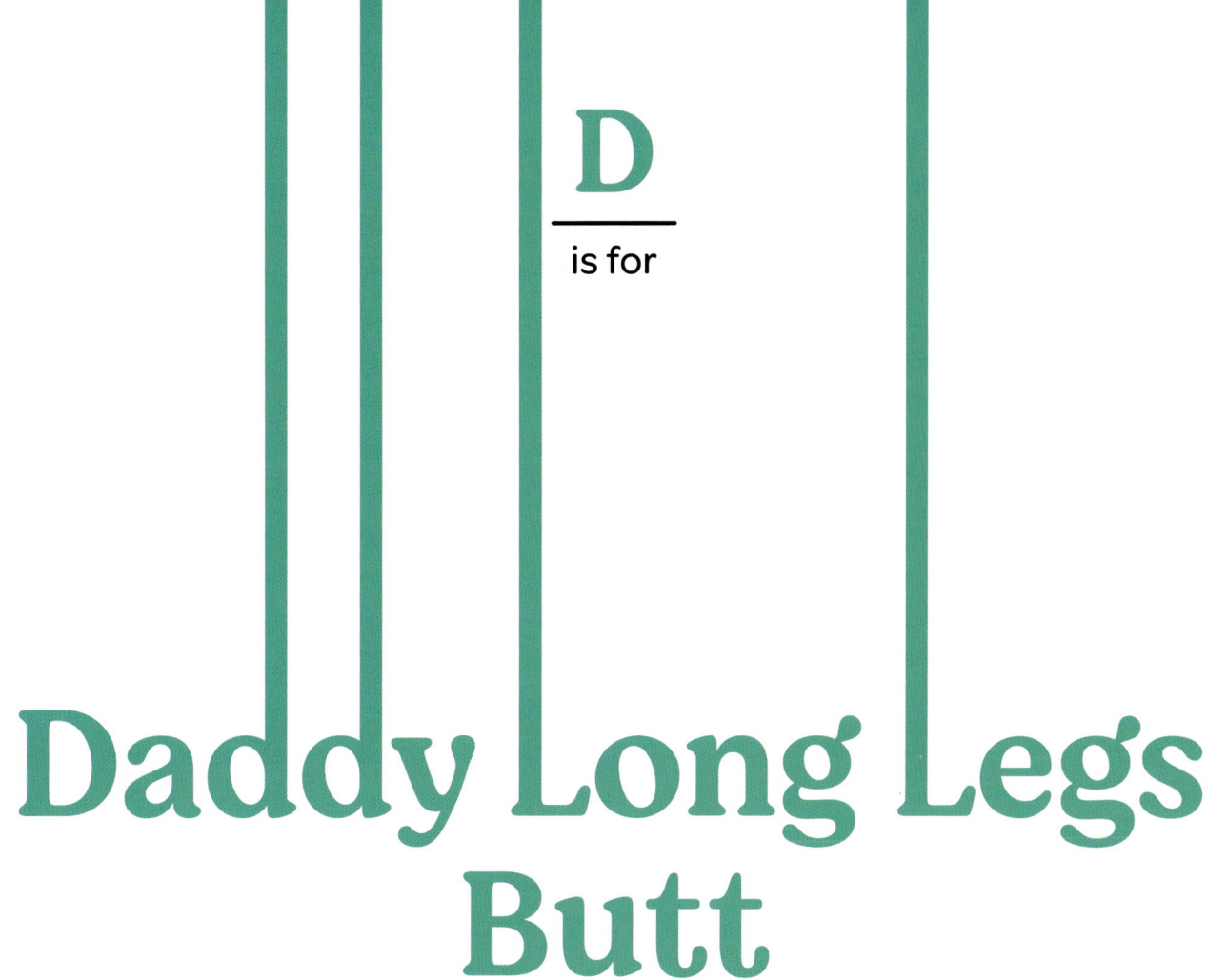

D is for

Daddy Long Legs Butt

Doing a dopey dance with daddy to disco ditties

Zachariah OHora • @fuzzytown

E

is for

Eggy Butt

Exhausting everyone with its endless energy

Christoph Niemann · @abstractsunday

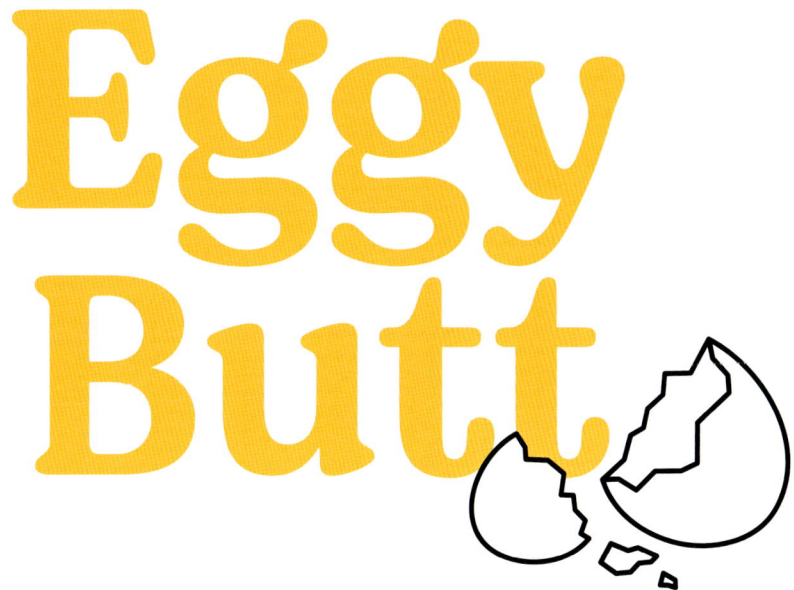

F
is for

Flamingo Butt

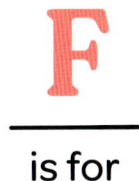

Frolicking freely with
its floppy feet

G
---
is for

Gigantasaurus Butt

Goofily galloping at the ginormous gymnasium

Jasmine Floyd • @jasminefloyd

is for

Herculean Butt

Hopping around saying "howdy" with its huge hands

is for

Itty
Bitty
Butt

Imagining it's impressively ice skating indoors

J
---
is for

Jiggly Jelly Butt

Jingle-jangling while
jumping joyously

Tyler Feder • @tylerfeder

is for

Known for its kooky karate kicks
and occasional K9 karaoke

L
is for

Lopsided Butt

Laughing while leaping into large lumps of laundry

Erika Lynne Jones • @erikalynnejones

M

is for

Munchkin Butt

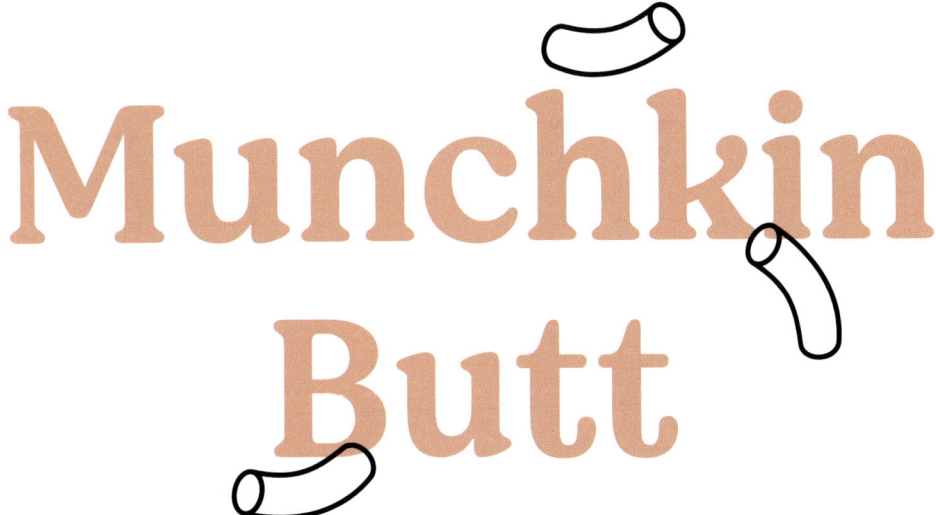

Moving merrily past Mommy while munching meatless mostaccioli

Tisha Lee · @tishalee_art

N
———
is for

No Butt Butt

Noisily going nutso in the nursery at naptime

is for

Old Man Butt

Outrunning other one-year-olds as onlookers say "oooooh"

P
is for

Pillowy Butt

Playfully pouncing upon
its pooped parents

is for

QUADRI LATERAL Butt

On a quest to become a highly-qualified quarterback queen

Jana Glatt • @janaglatt

R
is for

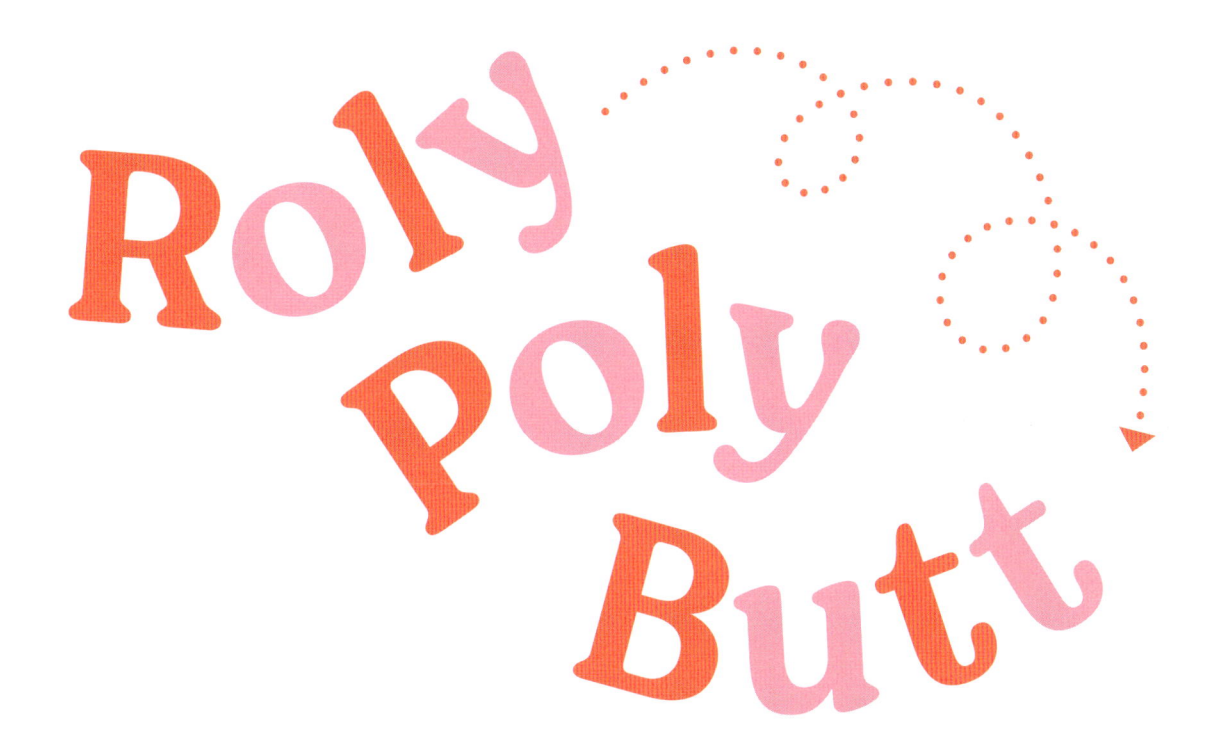

Roly Poly Butt

Rambunctiously rocking that rump round 'n' round

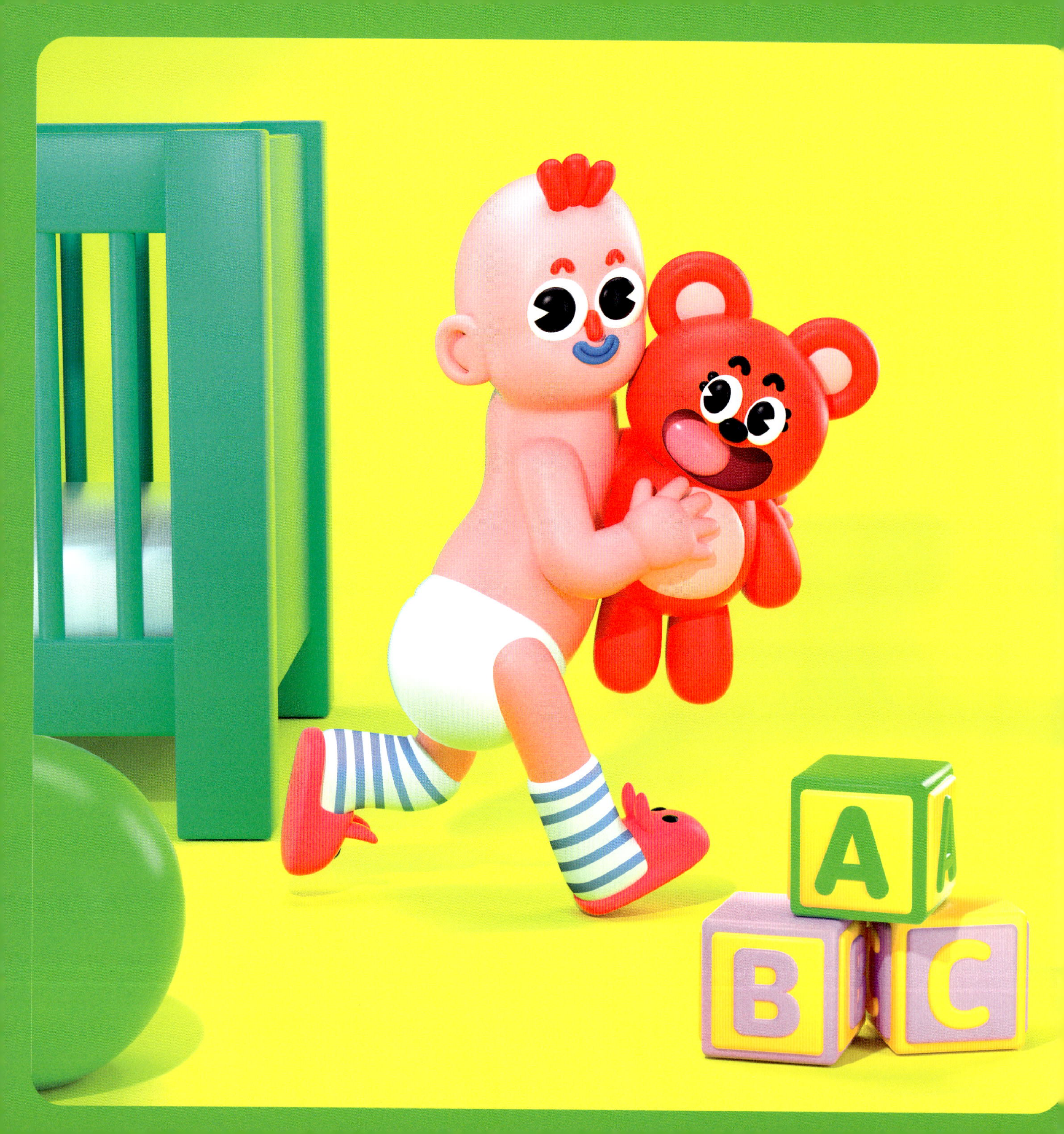
A
B
C

S
is for

String Beany Butt

Strutting like a silly-pants in super, stripy socks

Grand Chamaco • @grand_chamaco

Tater Tot
True Love
Love me
Boo!
PFFT
SNAKES LIKE TATERS
HOW MANY REVISIONS WILL GORDI MAKE ME DO?
L8RT8R
XOXO
POKE
YOU

T
is for

Tater Tot Butt

Twisting its tushy while tooting to and fro

Jason Grube • @grubedoo

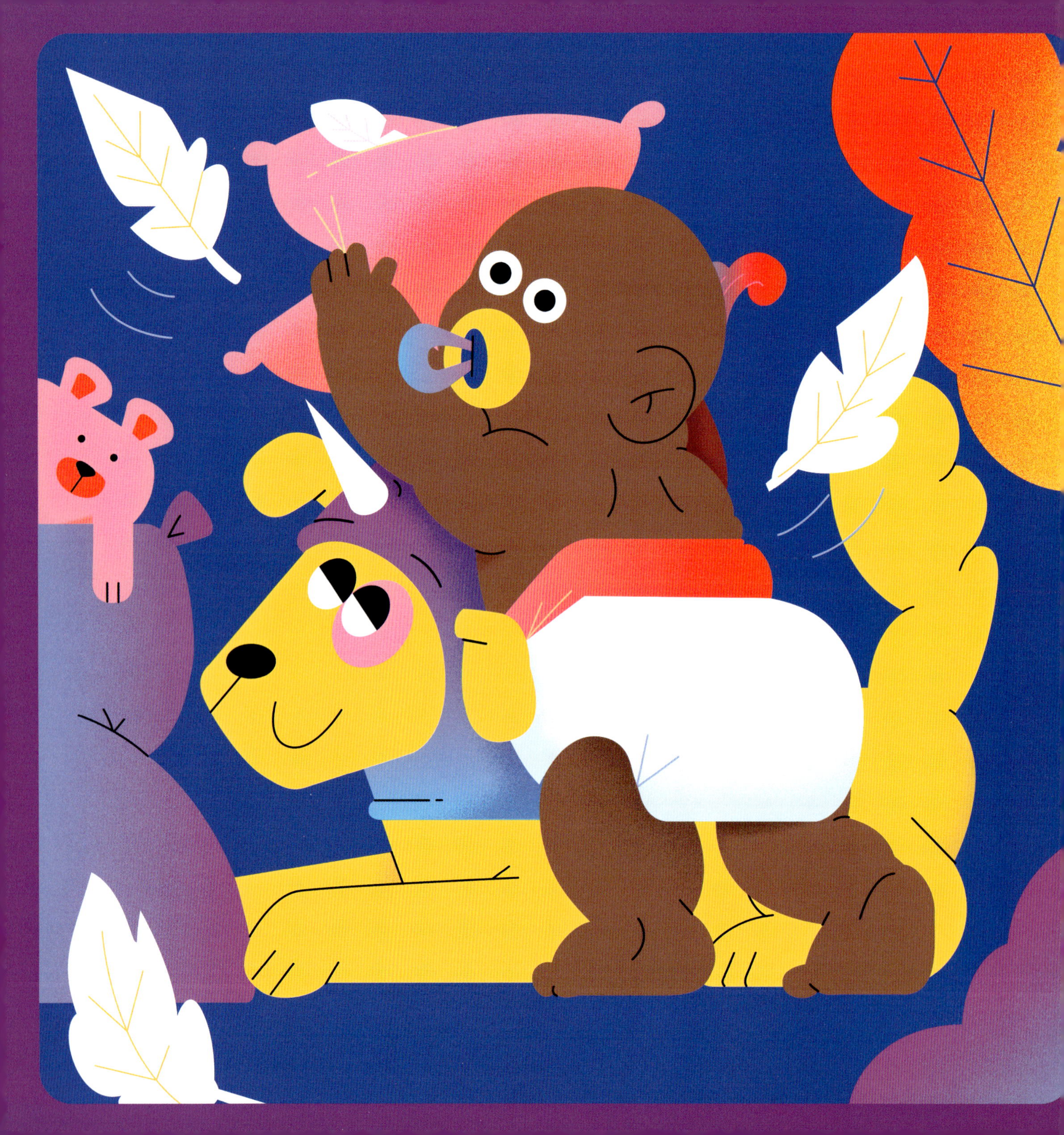

U
---
is for

Unicorn
Butt

Which, left unattended, may unfortunately upend all upholstery

Juan Molinet · @molinetjuan

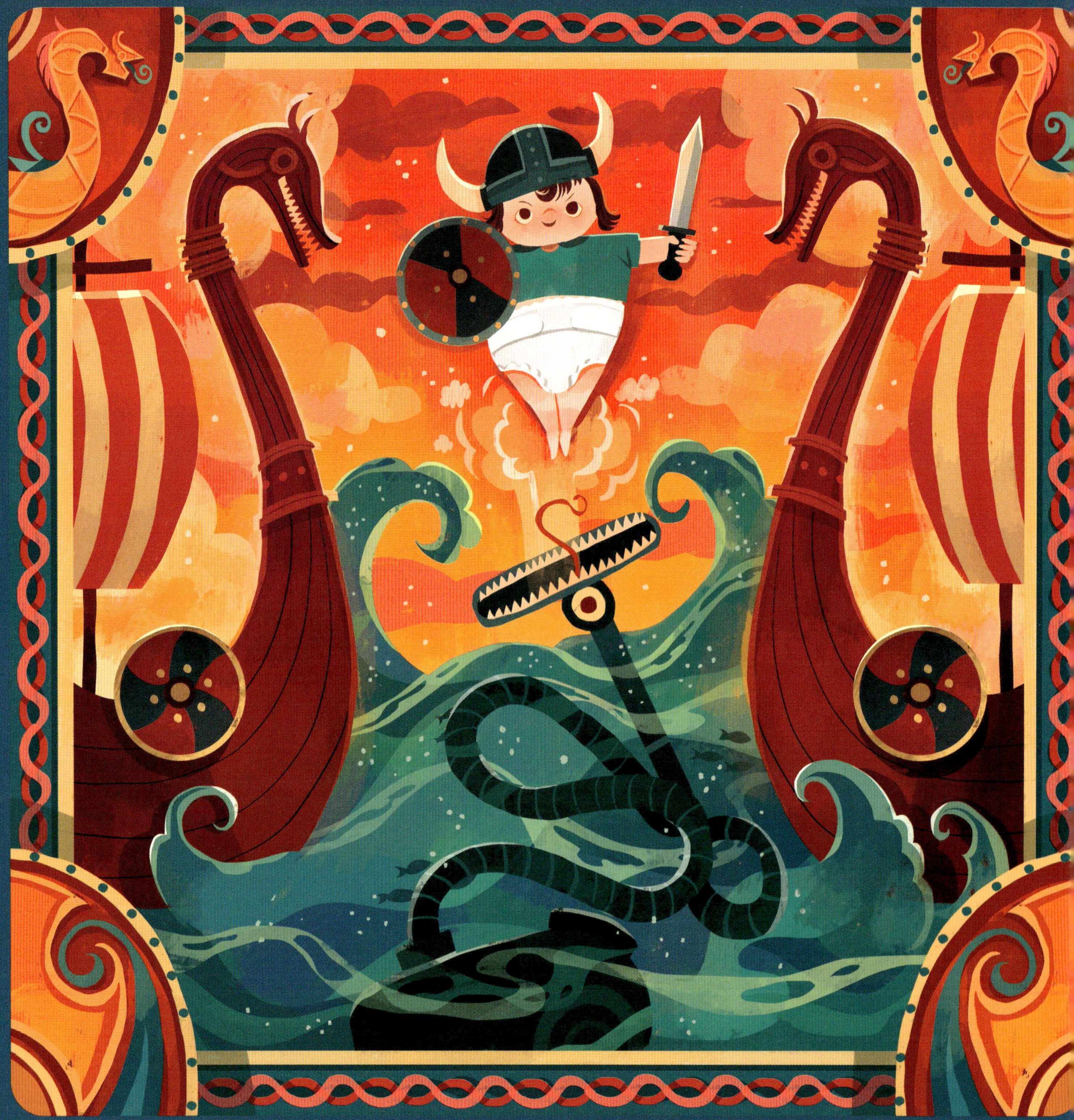

V
is for

Viking Butt

Vertically vaulting over a very loud-volume vacuum

Chaaya Prabhat · @chaaya23

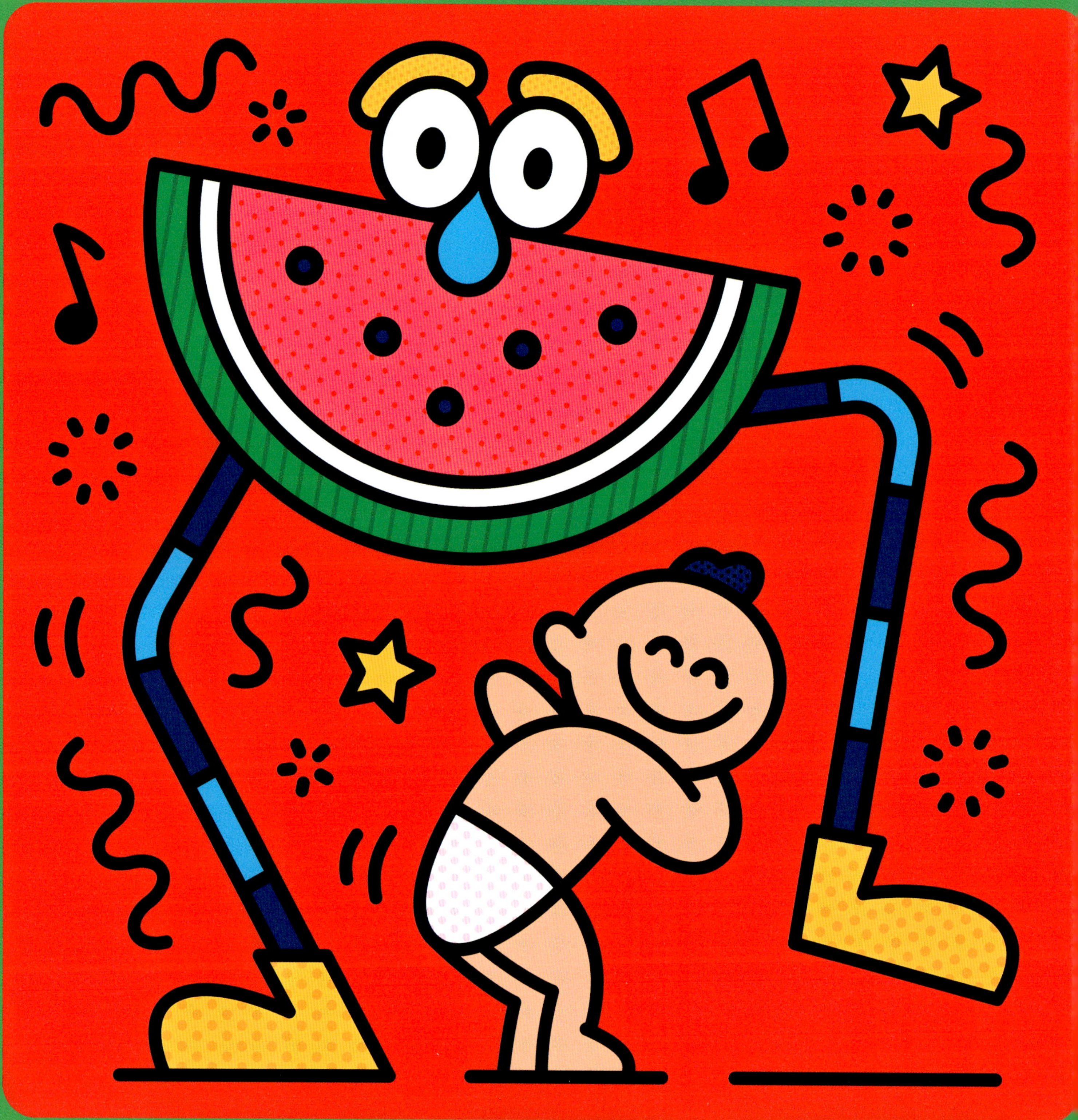

W
is for

W
E E
N S Y
Teensy Butt

Weirdly wiggly-waggling with a wedge of watermelon

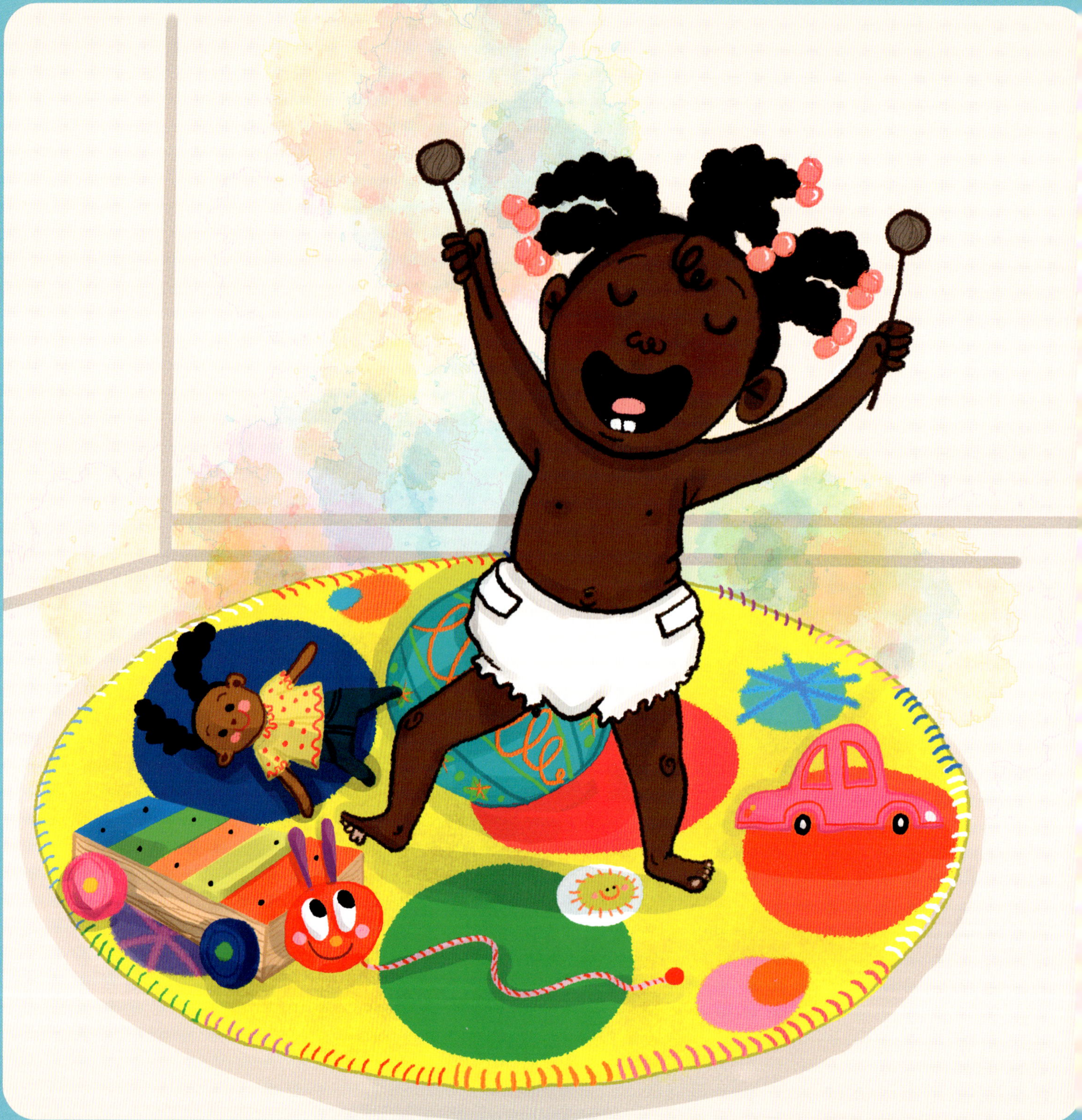

X
is for

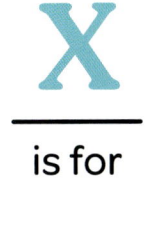

X-tra SQUISHY Butt

X-citedly x-pressing itself on the xylophone

Vanessa Brantley-Newton • @vanessabrantleynewton

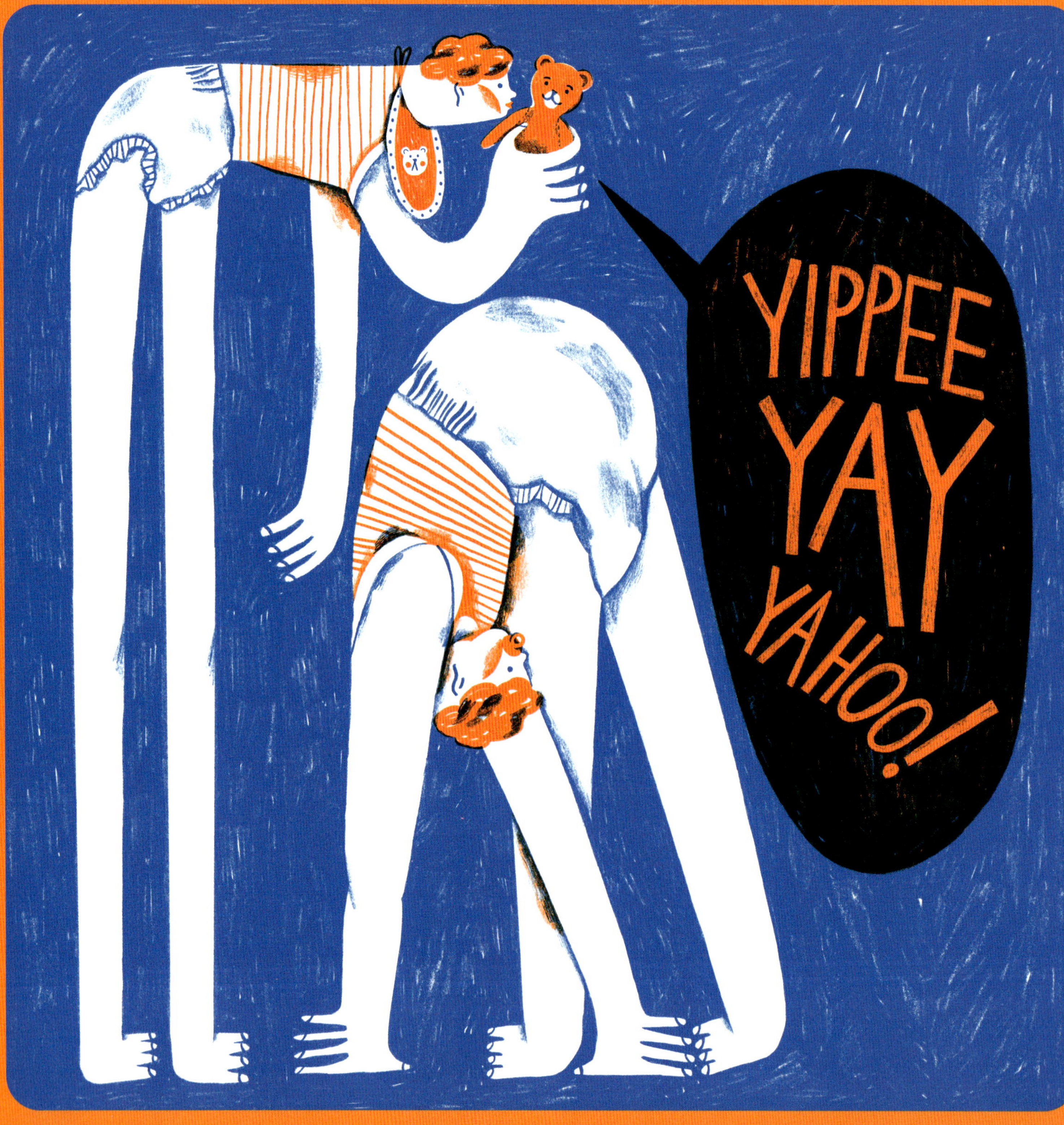
YIPPEE YAY YAHOO!

Y
is for

Yardstick Butt

Yoga-ing like a yo-yo while yammering "yippee yay yahoo!"

Alice Piaggio · @alicepiaggio_illustratrice

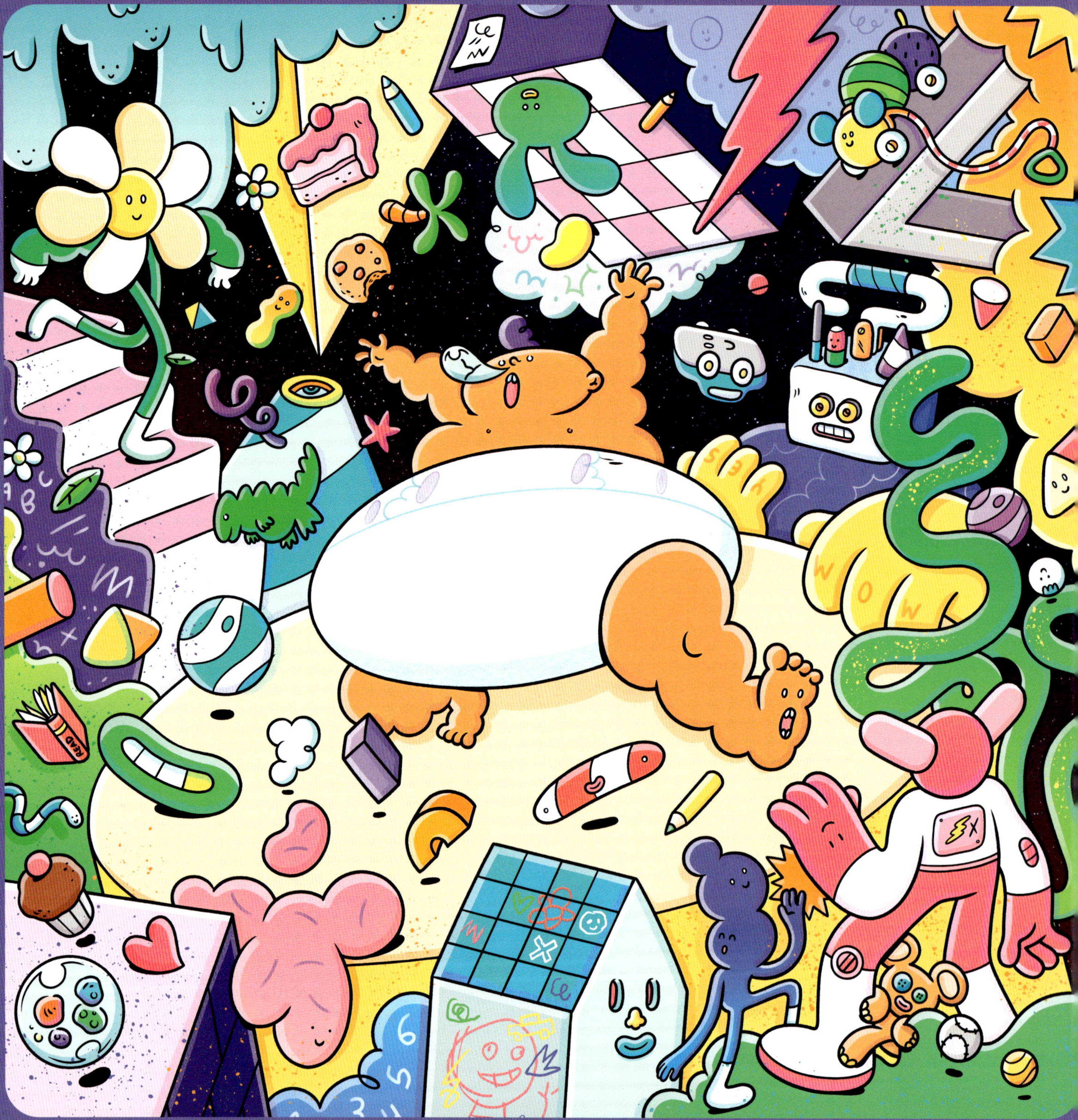
yes
WOW
READ

$\dfrac{\text{z}}{\text{is for}}$

Zeppelin Butt

Ziggin' and zaggin' like a zany, zonked-out zombie

Brosmind • @brosmind

Alphabutt Artists

Brought to you by HUGGIES

D Zachariah OHora @fuzzytown

E Christoph Niemann @abstractsunday

F Mathias Ball @sulkypup

J Tyler Feder @tylerfeder

K Flavia Z Drago @flavia_zdrago

L Erika Lynne Jones @erikalynnejones

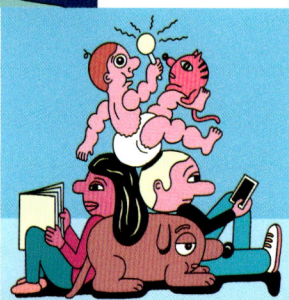

P Jeremyville @jeremyville

Q Jana Glatt @janaglatt

R Keith Negley @keith_negley

V Chaaya Prabhat @chaaya23

W Craig & Karl @craigandkarl

X Vanessa Brantley-Newton @vanessabrantleynewton

A Teresa Bellón @teresa_bellon

B Gemma Correll @gemmacorrell

C JooHee Yoon jooheeyoon.com

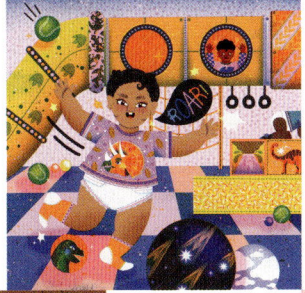

G Jasmine Floyd @jasminefloyd

H Christiane Engel @chengel_illustration

I Sarah Andersen @sarahandersencomics

M Tisha Lee @tishalee_art

N Heegyum Kim @hee_cookingdiary

O Elise Gravel @elise_gravel

S Grand Chamaco @grand_chamaco

T Jason Grube @grubedoo

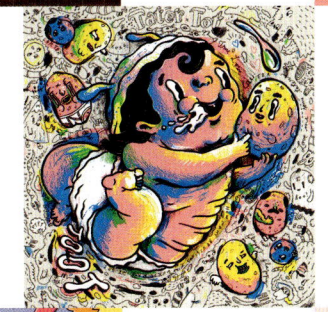

U Juan Molinet @molinetjuan

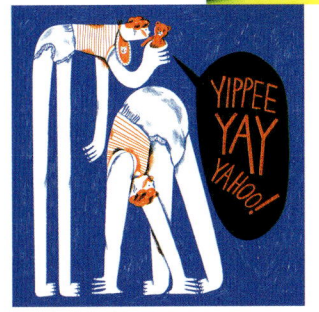

Y Alice Piaggio @alicepiaggio_illustratrice

Z Brosmind @brosmind

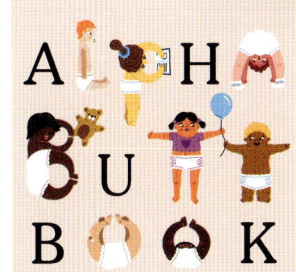

Cover Jason Grube @grubedoo

Leave No Butts Behind

Not only did we want to make a book about baby butts, but we also wanted to help cover every butt in need. So all proceeds of *The Alphabutt Book* go to the National Diaper Bank Network, a charity working to end diaper poverty by providing diapers to families in need. Because every baby butt in the world deserves to feel safe and cozy.

To learn more visit **nationaldiaperbanknetwork.org**

HUGGIES Project Hug X **National Diaper Bank Network**

The Alphabutt Book: an ABCs of Baby Butts & Bodies
Text and Illustrations Copyright © 2023 by Kimberly-Clark Worldwide, Inc.

Illustration credits: Teresa Bellon, Gemma Correll, JooHee Yoon, Zachariah Ohora, Christoph Niemann, Mathias Ball, Jasmine Floyd, Christiane Engel, Sarah Andersen, Tyler Feder, Flavia Z Drago, Erika Lynne Jones, Tisha Lee, Heegyum Kim, Elise Gravel, Jeremyville, Jana Glatt, Keith Negley, Grand Chamaco, Jason Grube, Juan Molinet, Chaaya Prabhat, Craig & Karl, Vanessa Brantley Newton, Alice Piaggio, Brosmind

No part of this publication may be reproduced, stored in a retrieval system or transmitted in any form by any means, electronic, mechanical, photocopy, recording, or otherwise, without the prior permission of the publisher, except for the use of quotations in articles or reviews, or as provided by US copyright law.

Hardcover ISBN 979-8-9880858-0-5
eBook ISBN 979-8-9880858-1-2

First Hardcover Edition

1 3 5 7 9 10 8 6 4 2

Concepted & written by QualityMeatsCreative.com
Editorial Consultation by Alli Brydon
Design by Headquarters.studio

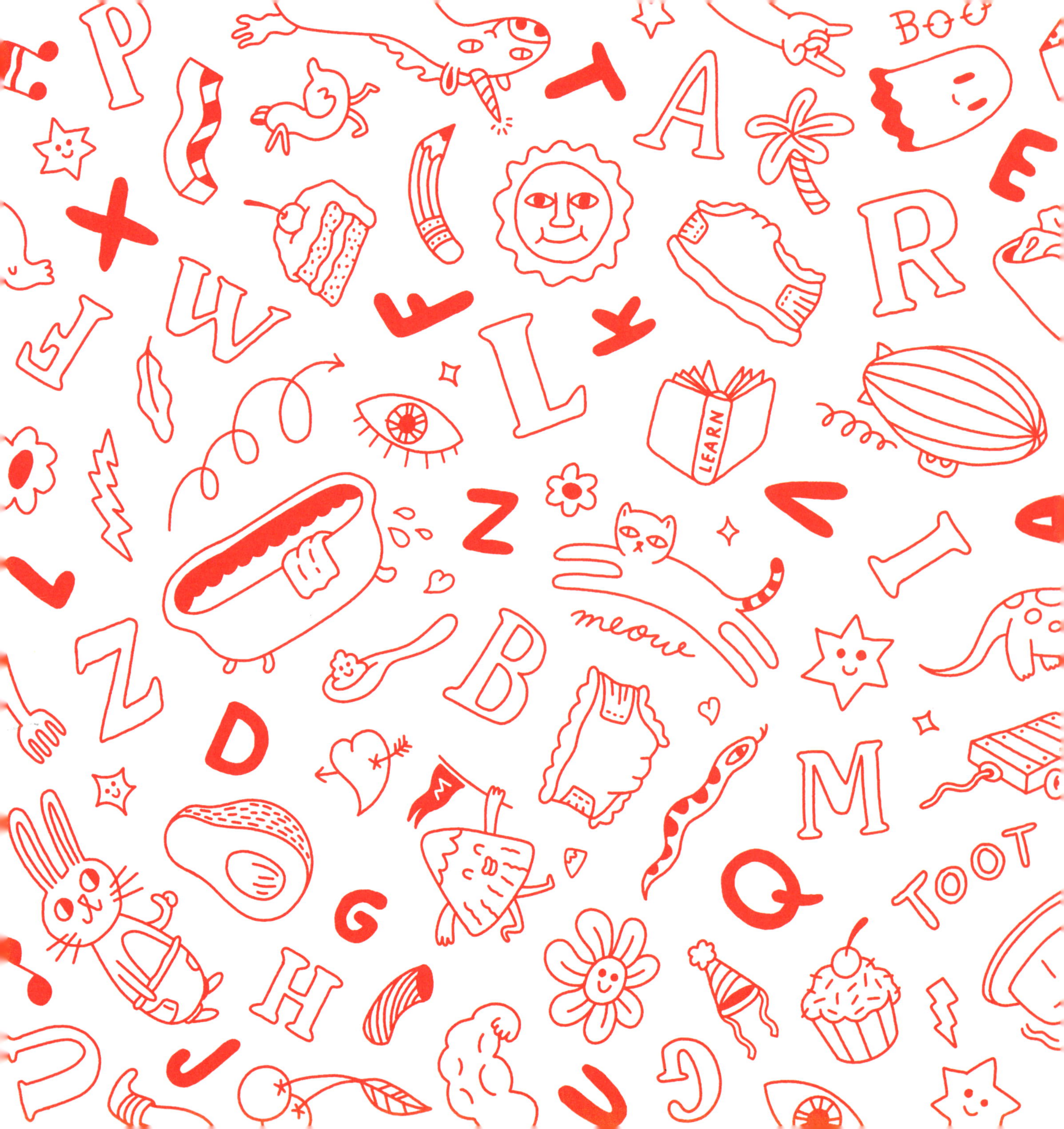
BOO
LEARN
meow
TOOT